To Mom,
thanks for saying yes.

Get the **FREE Coloring Book** at:
JolieCanoli.com/ButMomFreebies

Publishing

Published in the United States,
by Think Voyage Publishing LLC
203 Wilson Ave., West Bend, Wisconsin, 53090
Library of Congress Control Number: 2018914337
ISBN: 978-0-9996701-6-3
JolieCanoli.com

But Mom Said No!

Created by

Jolie Canoli and Jessica Ostrander

One sunny summer day, good friends met up to play.

Each kid had tales to tell of pets that could not stay.

They could not understand. How could their moms say no?

Despite their hopes and dreams, the beasts were made to go.

“My pet was from the sea,” said Jaxon with a frown,

“a squiggly wiggly guy, the cutest pet in town.

I found an empty fish bowl, but soon it seemed too small.

He grew, and as he grew, his arms could do it all!

His suction cups picked up, he even did my chores!

But Mom said 'No!' He had to go. I guess he broke the doors."

"Oh my, that's just so sad,"

said Ruby from her swing.

"My pet was in my house,

just hanging from a string.

She made a web or two.

She used her own supplies.

She stitched around my bed

a decorative surprise.

BUDD

She strung and hung up things. She spun her spinning spool.

But Mom said 'No!' She had to go. She made me late for school."

“It’s hard to say goodbye,” said Sam, as she recalled.

“My pet was just a snake. It ate a lot, that’s all.

It ate my sock and shoe. It ate a peach and plum.

It ate a pogo stick and chewed my chewing gum.

It ate a bike and sink; it wasn't all that weird.

But Mom said 'No!' It had to go

when grandma disappeared."

Then the kids were quiet, not sure of what to say.

Perhaps Sam's mom was right to send her pet away.

The kids all missed their pets, and Sam sure missed her snake.

But maybe it was best for Sam and Grandma's sake.

"I found my pet down south,"

said Peter from the slide.

"He didn't eat too much.

He didn't play outside.

He liked to be alone.

He liked to look at maps.

He liked to read and write—

a genius pet, perhaps!

He shook some slimy hands

with both his fins unfurled.

POLICE

But Mom said 'No!' He had to go.

He tried to rule the world."

“My pet was soft and fluffy,”

said Daisy way up high.

“She wasn’t big or scary.

She didn’t eat or spy.

She was cute and cuddly. So easy to adore.

My one and only pet...

...then two, then three, then more!"

My brother got an itch, and Mom began to sneeze.

My nose began to run, and Dad caught some disease.

But Mom and Dad, my great grandad,

our mailman Brad, and every neighbor

that I had said, 'No!' She had to go.

CAUTION
DANGER

POLICE

It really was too bad."

The sun was going down. It was the time to go.
The kids all hung their heads. So many moms say no.
To say goodbye is tough, it might feel sad and wrong.
But beasts should only live in places they belong.
The kids indeed were sad, but now they understood.
Mom sometimes says "No." And sometimes that is good.

But then they heard a sound, a “mew” came soft and sweet.

Five kittens, free for taking! Pets for moms to meet.

What would the moms all say?

The kids could only guess.

But deep inside they knew

this time it would be "Yes!"

The End.

But Mom Said, "Let's talk about it!" Conversation Starters

Each time you read this story you can choose a topic to start a meaningful conversation with your child. The "Extra mile" is a prompt to share a personal story. If it's bedtime and you're too tired, feel free to skip that one!

Reading Comprehension

1. Why did Mom say no about the octopus? The spider? The snake? The penguin? The dust bunny?
2. Do you think Mom will say yes about the kittens? Why or why not?
3. Even though it was best that Mom said "no," the kids were still sad. It's ok to be sad sometimes. Did the kids stay sad, or did their feelings change?

Being Told No

1. Sometimes we are told "no" because it keeps us safe, helps us be patient, or makes things better for us. Think of a time you were told no. Can you think of why it was better for you to be told "no"?
2. *Extra Mile* Let me share a time when I was told "no," and I learned that it was best for me.

Saying No

1. Sometimes kids need to say "no" too! Saying no to things that are bad for you is important. Can you think of something that you would need to say "no" to? (Examples: Saying no to eating too much candy, saying no to tricky adults or strangers, saying no to being mean to someone.)
2. Can you think of a time when you said "no" for a good reason?
3. *Extra Mile* It is important to say "no" when it keeps you safe and keeps others safe. I know you can be brave and say "no" if you need to. Let me tell you a story of a time that I had to be brave and say "no."

Download your fun freebies at:
JolieCanoli.com/ButMomFreebies

Jolie Canoli
(aka Dr. Jolie Williams) writes children's stories that knit humor and heart into learning. She first began writing stories for the stage. Now, as a mother of four adventurous kids, Jolie loves to create stories that stir children to think bigger and love better. She also composes music, draws illustrations, and performs internationally with her husband.

Jessica Ostrander
creates oodles of doodles bringing stories to life with vibrant creativity. She is a visual and performing artist, art and theater educator, and honorary Disney Imagineer. Her living persona of silliness brings joy on stage and off, entertaining kids of all ages. She believes stories are the key to making the world a better place because they help each of us discover a piece of ourselves and find where we belong.

*Schedule our **live children's show** featuring puppetry, original songs and theatrical storytelling at your local school or library!*

If you enjoyed this story you'll love Buddy Bones adventures too! Watch his vlog and get the puppet set at ***JolieCanoli.com***

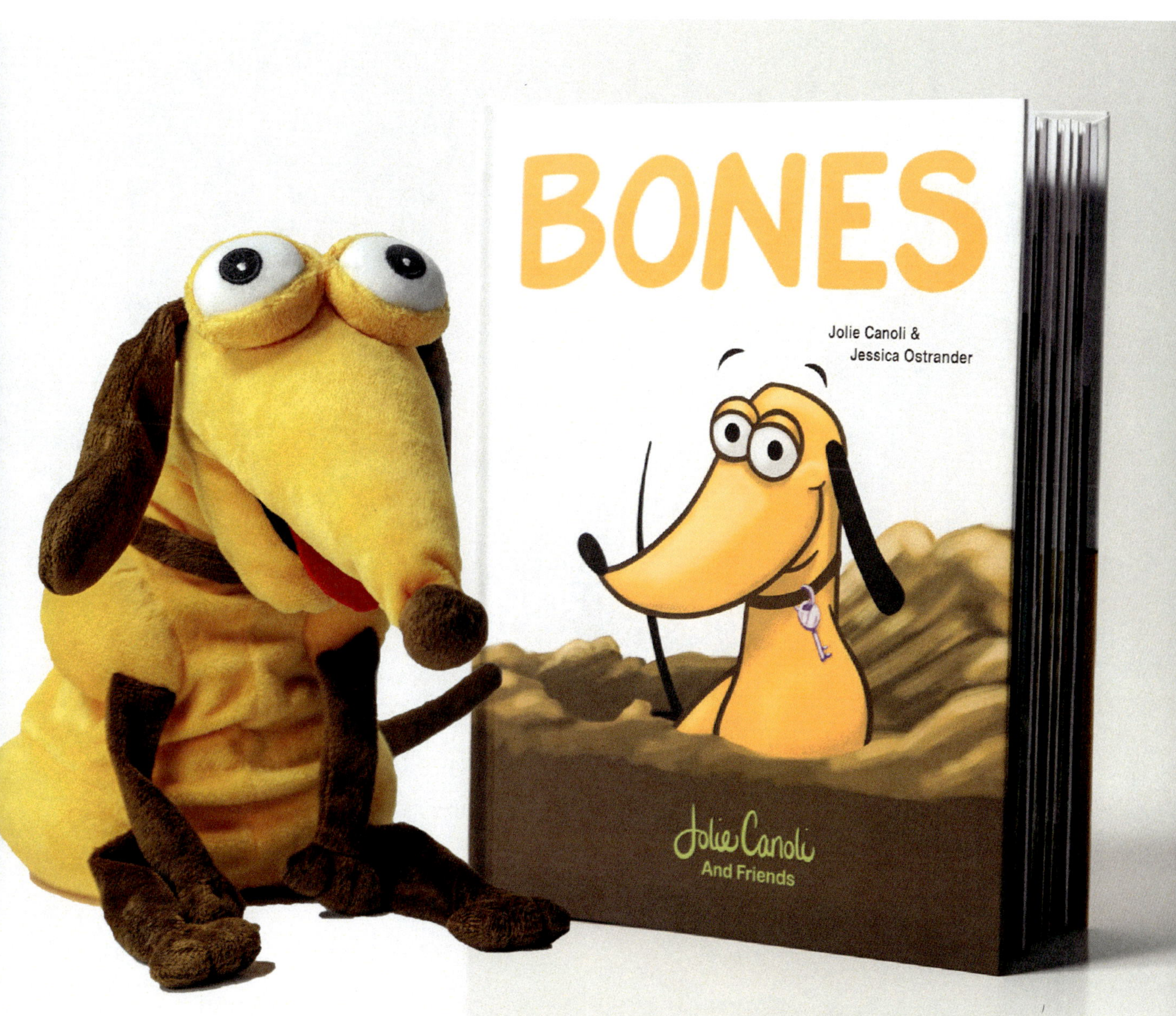

Made in the USA
Monee, IL
11 March 2024

54418052R00036